Carla at the Market

Written by Ian MacDonald

Illustrated by Veronica Montoya

Carla and her mum are off to the market.
Carla gets her jacket.

Carla and Mum are at Town Market.

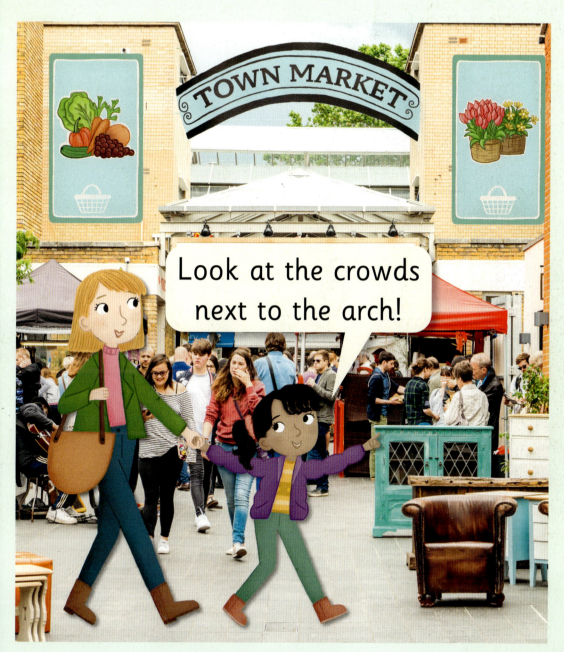

Carpets, rugs and towels are stacked high.

Can I get this towel for Dad?

This farm cart sells jars of jam.

We sell mustard, too!

JAM
MUSTARD

Can we get some jam?

Mum gets a trowel, a plant pot and a little garden fork.

Mum looks at bright gowns and silk saris.

Do you like this smart scarf?

In the yard, Mum and Carla sit down at a bench.

custard tarts

hot chicken

FOOD TRUCK

Now we can have lunch!

pakoras

PLEASE QUEUE THERE

Is it my turn to pick the street food?

Soon, the bus will come!

Carla looks hard. She spots a little brown fur fox.

Dad is in the garden when they get back.
He likes his towel!

Talk about the story

Ask your child these questions:

1 Which market stall did Carla and her mum visit first?

2 What did Carla say looked like a shark?

3 Why did Carla's mum tell her she needed to hurry at the toy stall?

4 Why do you think Carla asked if they could go back to the market?

5 What would you have bought at Town Market?

6 What kind of stall would you choose to run at a market?

Can your child retell the story in their own words?